P9-DDC-889

To: _____

From: _____

Why: _____

_____

Something Worth Leaving Behind

BRETT BEAVERS & TOM DOUGLAS

Introduction by
LEE ANN WOMACK

RUTLEDGE HILL PRESS™ · *Nashville, Tennessee*

A DIVISION OF THOMAS NELSON, INC.

For Liz—my true companion. Thank you for never thinking twice.
For Emily and Caleb—our two precious masterpieces ... in the works.
Thanks to Mom and Dad—who I am is because of you.
Thanks to Rick and Jim—for a lifetime of great memories ... and the ones yet to come
Thanks to Lorraine—for always being such a sweet inspiration.

—BRETT

To Katie—Thank you for dreaming with me. What a blast!
To Katherine, Claire, and Tommy—I pray your salt and light will make beautiful marks on this world.
To the boys on the hill, Gif and Anderson—Thanks for the inspirational miles.

—TOM

To Lee Ann: This song was a gift. Thank you for helping us share it with the world.

—BRETT and TOM

Published by Rutledge Hill Press, a Division of Thomas Nelson, Inc., P.O. Box 141000, Nashville, Tennessee 37214.

Photos on pages 7, 8–9, 14, 15, 23, 25, 41, 55, 57, 61, 62–63, 64, and back endsheet licensed through Dynamic Graphics/Creatas.
Photos on pages 18, 21, 28, 29, 32, 33, 34–35, 36, 37 licensed through Brand X Pictures.
Photos on front endsheet and pages 50, 51, 52–53 licensed through Corbis Images.
Photos on front & back covers, and pages 1, 24, 42–43, 56 licensed through Getty Images.
Photo on pages 54–55 licensed through Adobe Images.
Photos on pages 30–31, 45 licensed through ArtToday.
Photo on page 46 licensed through Digital Vision.
Photo on page 13 licensed through Image Club Graphics.
Photo on page 60 licensed through Index Stock.
Photo on page 47 licensed through Rubber Ball Images.

Cover & text design by Bruce Gore / Gore Studio, Inc.

ISBN: 1-4016-0032-8

Printed in the United States of America

02 03 04 05 — 6 5 4 3 2 1

Something Worth Leaving Behind

Hey Mona Lisa, who was Leonardo
Was he Andy Warhol, were you Marilyn Monroe
Hey Mozart, what kind of name is Amadeus
It's kind of like Elvis, you gotta die to be famous
I may not go down in history
I just want someone to remember me

I'll probably never hold the brush that paints a masterpiece
I'll probably never find the pen that writes a symphony
But if I will love then I will find
I have touched another life and that's something
Something worth leaving behind

Hey Midas, they say you had the magic touch
But even all that shiny stuff someday's gonna turn to dust
Hey Jesus, it must have been some Sunday morning
In a blaze of glory, we're still telling your story
I may not go down in history
I just want someone to remember me

I'll probably never dream a dream and watch it turn to gold
I know I'll never lose my life to save another soul
But if I will love then I will find
I have touched another life and that's something
Something worth leaving behind

Hey baby, see the future that we're building
Our love lives on in the lives of our children
And that's something
Something worth leaving behind

SEARCY GOTHARD

You won't hear his name mentioned among those such as Mozart, Midas, or Elvis. He was a man who thought little of money and the things it could buy. He believed in hard work and being kind to others. He owned one suit which he wore every Sunday and he held to simple beliefs that he passed down to each of his children...and grandchildren.

Searcy Gothard was my grandfather. He was an ordinary man who lived an extraordinary life by loving his family and always putting them first. He made each one of us feel smart, pretty, talented, important, safe...and most of all loved. He was an example to me of what we all can and should do in this world...leave a legacy...in the lives of those we love.

I believe that's something worth leaving behind.

LEE ANN WOMACK

You are about to read of
some of history's greatest people.
People like Leonardo da Vinci,
Wolfgang Amadeus Mozart, and Jesus.
Their stories are unforgettable.
The marks they made
on the world are indelible.
They left behind something
that has allowed them to live on
through history.
They gave us masterpieces . . .
symphonies . . .
a message of hope
and love.

da Vinci… Mozart… Jesus…

The reality is that most of us will never affect the world as they have.

But we each leave **amazing legacies** when we love those around us.

I may not go down in history
I just want someone to remember me

If I will love then I will find
I have touched another life and that's something
Something worth leaving behind

So remember,

As you move through the days
and years of your life,
you DO NOT go unnoticed.

You leave a trail, an impression, footprints . . .

unquestionable PROOF

that you existed . . .

in the lives of those around you.

8

Do you think you've not made much of a difference in this world? You have in mine.

Thank you.

Do you want to be remembered by those you've touched?

You can.

By showing love…
to one person at a time.

And that's something
Something worth
leaving behind.

"Hey *Mona Lisa,*
who was Leonardo?"

LEONARDO DA VINCI (1452–1519)

He was the illegitimate son of a peasant woman and Florentine merchant who became one of the greatest painters and most versatile geniuses the world has ever known.

He was a brilliant architect, engineer, military strategist, inventor, and scientist whose ideas and designs were centuries ahead of their time.

He was the creator of such masterpieces as
The Last Supper and *Mona Lisa.*
His influence lives on to this day in his paintings, writings, and sketches.

What was the secret of his greatness and genius?
He keenly observed the world around him and saw…

POSSIBILITIES.

When he looked at marble…
> he saw the sculpture.

When he looked at the sky…
> he saw flying machines.

When he looked at a church wall or a piece of wood or a blank canvas…
> He saw *The Last Supper,*
> He saw *Mona Lisa,*
> He saw

masterpieces.

WHAT IS A
masterpiece?

A masterpiece is a gift to the world

from the one who conceives it,

labors over it, and then…

leaves it behind for all

the world to see.

A reminder…

of the beauty one person can create.

And we gaze upon it and wonder…

Could I create a masterpiece?

Maybe not in OIL…

Maybe not in BRONZE…

Maybe not in MARBLE.

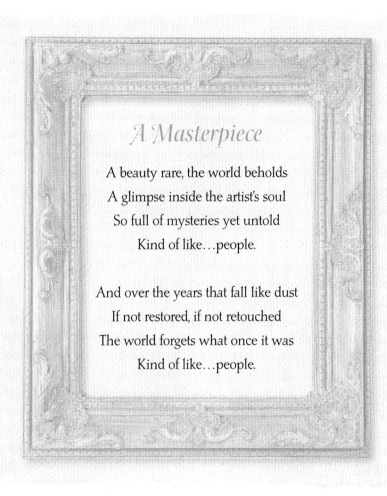

A Masterpiece

A beauty rare, the world beholds
A glimpse inside the artist's soul
So full of mysteries yet untold
Kind of like…people.

And over the years that fall like dust
If not restored, if not retouched
The world forgets what once it was
Kind of like…people.

Think about the people in YOUR WORLD.
You have the opportunity every day to make their lives…

MORE BEAUTIFUL

For having known…YOU. That's really something…

Something
worth
leaving
behind.

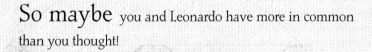

So maybe you and Leonardo have more in common
than you thought!

For when you reach out and touch another life,

YOU make a lasting impression.
YOU leave your brush strokes in
the lives of those around you…

And I believe someone
will think of you and say…

"I am a canvas

Have been all my life
Will be until I'm gone

At one time in my life you touched me,
Carefully. And made your mark…

A shade of RED
When I was weary and losing my passion.
A splash of BLUE across my sky
When the world looked gray and gloomy.
Some easy GREENS
When my soul was thirsty…

For the promise of spring.
For second chances,
For forgiveness.

You may not have known you were doing it,
  But I did…
      AND I WILL REMEMBER.

Do you think you've not made much of a difference in this world?
You have in mine.
THANK YOU.

  I am a canvas
  One day…

A MASTERPIECE."

                              So remember…

YOU are the artist who paints a masterpiece
In the lives of those around you.

Maybe you are doing it right now.
Maybe you will do it tomorrow,
Or the day after that.

But you WILL make a difference.
You'll make a beautiful difference.

With words of encouragement,
Words of hope.
With a smile…
A long hug…
A heart felt "thank you."

There are CANVASES...

All around you.

Some are in desperate need of what only you can offer.

Awaken the artist within yourself and

PAINT

A masterpiece?
Yes...
A living, breathing, *masterpiece!*
How?

One person at a time,
One stroke at a time,
With the color of...

LOVE.

"Hey Mozart, what kind of name is Amadeus?"

I guess he would say it's Austrian, since that's where he was born. Actually, his whole name is pretty cool…

WOLFGANG AMADEUS MOZART (1756–1791)

Mozart is considered to be one of the most creative musical geniuses of all time.

Check out this timeline:

Age 4 ∾ He shows remarkable musical talent and learns to play the piano.

Age 5 ∾ He begins composing music.

Age 6 ∾ He plays for Empress Maria Theresa of Austria.

Age 14 ∾ He has already composed many works for the harpsichord, piano, and violin, as well as orchestral works.

Early 20s ∾ He is virtually ignored by the courts of Europe.

But Mozart presses on under difficult circumstances and composes his most enduring work during the later years of his life.

THEN *Age 35* ∼ He dies in poverty from a feverish illness and is buried in a Vienna suburb with little ceremony… in an unmarked grave.

Yet Mozart lives on to this day in the more than six hundred works of music he left behind.

What was the secret to his greatness and genius? He listened with his heart and heard…

POSSIBILITIES.

When he saw a violin…
　　　　　he heard concertos.

When he stood in an empty concert hall…
　　　　　he heard angels singing.

When he looked at a blank manuscript…

　　　he heard symphonies.

WHAT IS A
symphony?

A symphony is a gift to the world
from the one who conceives it,
labors over it, and then…
*leaves it behind for all
the world to hear.*

A reminder…
of the beauty one person can create.

Violins, cellos, basses.
Woodwinds and brass.
Percussion.

Working together like…

the beating

of a HEART.

The slow introduction
The rising of the second movement
The crescendo to the grand finale.
(Kind of like…life)

THEN…

The crowd flows out into the street
Lifted…
Above the noise of jackhammers and
　　　　horns and sirens.

Floating along on an
echo… echo… echo…

Of the music made
Of the precious memories
Of the life lived.

Think about the people in YOUR WORLD.

Someone in your life has been…
is now…will be…

LISTENING

For that missing part that can add much
needed wings to their life song.

Ears strained… for that faint sound of
"I love you…"
"You can do it…"
"You are important to me."

You can do that.

That's really something…
Something
worth
leaving
behind.

Seize those opportunities to lift someone up with **your** music... **your** life song.

For when you reach out
And touch another life,

You fill up the emptiness.
You create melody and harmony

on the pages of someone's heart.

And I believe someone will think of you and say...

"I am a song

Have been all my life
Will be until I'm gone.

Did you know that the music you wrote in
my soul long ago still reverberates inside
of me?

A melancholy tune for moments of
REFLECTION... *for who I was*

A joyous melody when I needed
CELEBRATION... *for who I was becoming*

An anthem to call my own when I needed
INSPIRATION... *for who I could be*

And a REST...
Just at the right time
Just in the right place.

In your humble way you did it
Without wanting any recognition or thanks

I REMEMBER.

Do you think you've not made much of a
difference in this world?
You have in mine.
Thank you.

I am a song
One day…

A SYMPHONY."

So remember…

YOU are the composer who writes a symphony
In the lives of those around you.

The Conductor's hand has dropped,
Leading the world in a
Harmonious parade of sound.

Make sure YOU are heard…
in the ears of those you love.

Never miss a chance to

Say "I love you."
　　　Remember someone's name.
　Sing a lullaby.
　　　Make someone laugh.

Now that's sweet, sweet music!

The composer inside of you is waiting to write.

A symphony?
You bet.
A living, breathing *symphony*.
How?

One person at a time,
One note at a time,
With the melody of…

LOVE.

For if you will love
Then you will find
You have touched
Another life

And that's something…

something

worth

leaving

behind.

"Hey *Midas,*
they say you had the magic touch."

As a reward for an act of kindness, the mythological King Midas
was granted by the Greek god Dionysus

ONE WISH…

Midas wished that everything he touched would turn to gold.
So, he began touching…

A flower…GOLD! He was rich…
A stone…GOLD! He was richer…
Anything and everything turned to GOLD!
He was the richest person on earth!

Or was he?

The food that touched his lips turned to gold…
and left him hungry.
The daughter he reached to hold turned to gold…
and left him heartbroken.

Realizing the mistake he had made, Midas begged to be free of his wish. After bathing in the River Pactolus, the curse was lifted. He then bathed his daughter in the river…and she was restored.

He had his daughter back.
He was no longer hungry.
He was no longer heartbroken.
He was no longer alone.

He was free!
Free to TOUCH…
Free to FEEL.

Now he was truly… rich.

The Road to Riches

Win the lottery
Receive an inheritance
Pass go and collect $200

or

Earn a little more than you spend…
(And keep doing it).

If you had one wish…
(It's fun to think about, isn't it?)
Here's mine for you…

That you would realize
in many ways
you are already

RICH!

Do you have two good eyes…
To see the gold in a sunrise,
The smile of a child catching his first fish,
The colors of a rainbow?

Do you have two strong arms…
To applaud a home run or a graduation,
To hug a parent or rock a baby,
To pull someone out of a burning building?

Do you have two strong legs…
To walk and run and dance,
To swim in the ocean,
To make angels in the snow?

Some people don't.

What else is on your list of riches?
I'll bet it's a long list.

Take a moment and…

COUNT YOUR BLESSINGS.

Then…

Think about the people in YOUR WORLD.

There have been moments when you
invested yourself in someone else's life.
Call them your MAGIC MOMENTS…

Magic moments are life's little
appointments when even the smallest act of
kindness can make someone feel like…
A million bucks!

Simple gestures…like pennies
That over someone's lifetime add up
To something that satisfies their deepest hunger…
That lets them know they are valuable
     To someone…
     To anyone…
     To you.

That's really something…
          Something
               worth
                    leaving
                         behind.

So, do you want to
feel rich?
Really rich?

Give yourself
To those around you.
They need you.

And you will get back in return what money can't buy…
A legacy that will live on in the lives of those you touch…
those you love.

And I believe someone will think of you and say…

"I am a treasure chest

Have been all my life
Will be until I'm gone.

At one time in my life you gave me
something priceless…
Yourself…your time.

You gave me…

Pearls of wisdom
When I needed guidance

Precious moments of affection
That still warm me to this day

And, oh those memories…
GOLDEN.

It may have seemed insignificant to you,
but to me it was worth more than you know.

You may not have known you were doing it
    But I did
        AND I STILL REMEMBER.

Do you think you've not made much of a
difference in this world?
You have in mine.

    I am a treasure chest,
    One day…

A TREASURE."

So remember…

YOU can watch a life turn to gold.

You don't have to be rich as King Midas
to be remembered.

Whenever you use . . .

YOUR TIME
to volunteer

YOUR TALENTS
to lend a helping hand

YOUR MONEY
to help someone in need

You create those MAGIC MOMENTS
that someone will never forget.

And you just might be starting a chain reaction that will still
be affecting the lives of people one hundred years from now…

That's a wonderful gift to the world.

So, can you turn something to gold?
Yes!

What?
The dreams and lives
of those around you.
How?
By giving…

One person at a time
    One reach at a time
        With the touch of…

            LOVE.

"Hey *Jesus,*
we're still telling your story."

Down through the past two thousand years,

the story of Jesus, the Son of God, has effected more

change in the human race than all the laws ever

passed and all the inventions of the human mind

put together.

HOW did Jesus Christ, in three short years,

forever change the course of humanity?

With a handful of ordinary followers,

AND . . .

A message
of love and acceptance,
of a kingdom…

A compassion
That draws men and women to Him
from all walks of life,

A sacrifice
of His own life that bridged the gap
between man and God.

The Open Arms of Love

When the children crowded around Him, He said,
"Let them come unto me…"
With open arms.

When the blind and the lame and the hungry
called His name, He healed and fed them…
With open arms.

When the world turned its back on Him and screamed
"Crucify!" He didn't run or hide. He let them drive nails
in His hands…
With open arms.

While He was dying on the cross and they mocked Him
and gambled for His garments, He prayed for them…
With open arms.

When He finished what He had come to earth to do,
He gave up His spirit and died…
With open arms.

After He rose from the grave, He found His friend who
had denied even knowing Him, and forgave him…
With open arms.

And when He left this world, He left…
With open arms.

During the twenty centuries that have come and gone, nation has warred against nation, new lands have been discovered, old societies have been conquered, and new ones have risen up in this ever-changing world in which we live.

Yet one thing has never changed…
Through it all, Jesus has given comfort, acceptance, and peace to those who call on Him…
With open arms.

And when His believers' time on this earth is done, He will welcome us home to a place called Heaven…
With open arms.

Think about the people in YOUR WORLD.

There will be opportunities every day
for you to open your arms…
      To the ones you love…
      To the strangers you don't know.

They just might see a light in you that will give them a
reason to believe in something bigger than themselves…
      Someone bigger than us all.

    That's really something…
        Something
          worth
            leaving
              behind.

You come from a long line of believers.

Believers in grace,

Believers in joy,

Believers in hope.

In the simplest ways, you can continue the chain of love started so long ago.

And I believe someone will think of you and say…

"I am a mortal

Have been all my life
Will be until I'm gone.

At one time in my life you whispered
forever in my ear...

The meaning of LIFE...
The beauty of LOVE...
The promise of HEAVEN...

You told me about a river...the river of life,
so that I would never thirst again.

You may have offered only a kind word,
a Bible verse...a prayer...
but my journey would have been more
difficult without you.

You may not have known
you were doing it.
   But I did.
      I STILL REMEMBER.

Do you think you've not made much
of a difference in this world?
You have in mine.
THANK YOU.

      I am a mortal,
      One day…

IMMORTAL."

                        So remember…

You can save another soul

From giving up hope…
From giving up on themselves…
From believing that this life on earth is all there is.

Maybe you are doing it right now.
Maybe a seed you planted long ago
has forever changed the course of someone's life.
Maybe your greatest moment is yet to come!

When someone's world is crumbling,
YOU can be their rock…

When someone has been crippled by the disappointments of life,
YOU can offer healing words of comfort and encouragement…

When someone's self belief has died,
YOU can help bring it back to life.

Draw from that river of life and
quench another's thirst for
something that

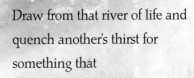

lasts forever.

Can you do something of
eternal significance?
Yes.
How?
By spreading grace, joy, and hope…

One person at a time
One word at a time
With the open arms of…

LOVE.

For if you will love

Then you will find

You have touched

Another life

And that's something…

something

worth

leaving

behind.

"Hey *baby*,
see the future that we're building."

THE FUTURE…

They say it's out there somewhere.
I'd say they're right.

It's out there in someone's arms tonight,
being rocked to sleep…
It's out there holding on to a sofa,
struggling to take those first steps…
It's out there sitting in a second grade classroom,
learning how to spell…
It's out there in a Sunday school class,
singing "Jesus loves me this I know…"
It's out there leaving home for the first time,
going off to college…

The future is out there being born every day and
every night in every city in the world…

Yes, the future is already here…

It's just young.

But it won't stay young forever…
It grows up a little more every day.
And one day it will take its place in a
coming present age and carve out its
own place in history.

So, while the future is still with us…WITH YOU…

YOU decide what to instill in it

YOU decide what it will look like

when it grows up.

This is our greatest calling…

Think about the children
in YOUR WORLD.

Maybe you tuck them in bed at night.
Maybe they are in your classroom.
Maybe they are on the team you coach

Never forget when you look into their eyes, you are looking into the eyes of

THE FUTURE.

You CAN have an impact on the future…
by reaching out and loving a child.

That's really something…
Something
worth
leaving
behind.

56

So go ahead…

change the future.

Dare children to dream…to explore…to try
And when they fall, to get up and go on.
Let them be their uniquely created selves.
Ask them "what if?"
Foster their awesome powers of

imagination…

Raise them up in an environment of

love and acceptance…

Never miss a chance to say

"I love you."

You will be having a direct impact on
THE FUTURE.

And I believe someone
will think of you and say…

"I am a child

In some ways, have been all my life
Will be until I'm gone.

At one time in my life you nurtured me
and made your mark.

You may have only wiped a tear
or sung me to sleep
or given me a call
or taught me a simple lesson about life.

But the person I'm becoming
would never have been complete
without YOU.

You may not have known you were doing it.
But I did…

I STILL DO.

Do you think you've not made much of a
difference in this world?
You have in mine.
THANK YOU.

I am a child,
One day…

THE FUTURE."

So remember…

Out there somewhere is our next president…
sitting in a fifth grade classroom.

Out there somewhere is the next great
mind like Leonardo da Vinci…
wondering how a tricycle works.

Out there is the next musical genius like Mozart…
playing "Twinkle, Twinkle Little Star" on
the piano for the first time.

Out there is our next generation of:
Teachers
Film directors
Newspaper editors
Talk show hosts
Farmers
Police officers
Actors
Lawyers
Statesmen…

And mothers…
(God bless the mothers)
And fathers.

THE FUTURE...
It's in your hands,
in our hands.
One day they will grow up
and go out into the world
to make their mark, make their difference.
And their children will do the same.
Here lies the unbreakable thread that runs
from past generations into You...
and down future generations from You.

Change the future...
Build the future...
How?

One moment at a time

One child at a time

With the promise of

LOVE.

I may not go down in history . . .
         I just want someone
                       to remember me.

This book has been somewhat of a
roll call of greatness . . .

> *Leonardo da Vinci*
> *Amadeus Mozart*
> *King Midas*
> *Jesus*

This is obviously only a partial list.
Many more names belong on the list,
and new names are being added
every day.

Names of everyday people who are
making a difference in their world.

Names like yours.

You may not create the types of masterpieces Leonardo did, the types of symphonies Mozart did, amass the great fortune King Midas did, or make the impact on humanity that Jesus did . . . and still does.

But I believe you belong in their company because of the legacy you are leaving in the lives of those around you.

By painting . . . with the color of love

By writing . . . with the melody of love

By touching . . . with the gift of love

By reaching . . . with the open arms of love

By changing the future . . . with the promise of love.

Do you think you've not made much of a difference in this world?

You have

Because . . .

"To know even one life has breathed easier because you have lived. This is to have succeeded."

—RALPH WALDO EMERSON

That's something …

Something

worth

leaving

behind.

Has someone made a difference in your life?

Telling your story might be a way of
making a difference in someone else's
life. We would like to hear about it and
perhaps share your story with others.

Send us an e-mail with your story of
how someone made a difference in
your life by going to our website:
www.SomethingWorthLeavingBehind.com.